From Stagnation to Restoration:

The Journey to Servanthood

By Rhonida A. Carter and Randryia L. Houston

© 2017 Rhonida A. Carter and Randryia L. Houston
All Rights Reserved

ISBN-13: 978-0-9914314-3-4

The credit of these writings goes to God and Him alone.

You will not know the extent of what you signed up for until you step into it.

Table of Contents

Introduction
    The Process to Truth   6

The Walk
    Anointing   10
    Prayer   12
    Fasting   14
    Vulnerability   16
    Perseverance   19
    Deliverance   22
    A Covenant   24
    Restoration   25

A 21-Day Devotional Journey to Restoration
    Day 1: Confess Your Faith   27
    Day 2: Accept the Past   28
    Day 3: Practicing Faith   29
    Day 4: Embracing God's Strength   30
    Day 5: Perspective   32
    Day 6: Love   33
    Day 7: Repentance   34
    Day 8: Obedience   35
    Day 9: Sensitive to the Spirit   36
    Day 10: Leave Space for God   37
    Day 11: Self-Examination   38
    Day 12: Thicker than Blood   39
    Day 13: Works in Progress   40
    Day 14: Staying Focused   41
    Day 15: Get Out There   42
    Day 16: Facing Our Fears   43
    Day 17: In the Darkness   44
    Day 18: Family in Christ   45
    Day 19: When No One's Watching   46

Day 20: Releasing Entitlement 47
Day 21: God Deserves the Glory 48

Conclusion 49
My Prayer for You 50
Acknowledgements 51
About the Authors 53

The Process to Truth

For the past two years, I have been studying Queen Esther and her journey from unknown to Queen. In reading Chapter 3 of *God Chasers*, Tenney's description of Esther's process took me deeper into her experience. I compare my Minister in Training (MIT) process to the Esther's experience, a year-long experience in preparation for one night with the King. It is to ensure that when the encounter happens, we will be in the correct posture of obedience, submission, and humility. Tenney describes Esther as enduring a "soaking process designed to turn a peasant into a princess".

Like Esther, I feel like my identity is hidden while being groomed and trained. As I become more exposed in gifts, talents, and anointing, I ask God to uncover me slowly. I know that there are people who smell the oil and perfume in which I have been soaked and seek to deter me from my ultimate assignment.

Esther and I share the privilege of having a wise mentor, who instructs and guides me through the training process. Like Esther, I have been adopted, raised as a daughter and prepared for greatness. In John 10, Jesus describes himself as the Good Shepherd who leads his sheep, sacrifices his life, and walks ahead of them. His sheep only listen to His voice. This is the relationship Esther had with Mordecai and the relationship MIT training is developing for me.

Also like Esther, I have the responsibility for fasting and praying for not only my life, but also for those in the kingdom. I have the ability and authority to save the lives of those with whom I commune and love. Esther sacrificed one year of her life, ensuring readiness for her destiny. As Esther was marred and molded, for the enlargement of her territory, as I hope I shall be as well.

The unraveling of the yarn is necessary to add another layer to my truth. One does not instantly arrive at her truth. It is a process, an evolving narrative, a working document. It is during times of fasting and praying that God shock slaps us to a bitter truth. We must seek him further to understand and accept this truth. My truth must move past a wavering belief to sustain me for the battle ahead. Strengthen our walls, Father.

During prayer, I saw myself being escorted onto a stage in a stadium of thousands of people. I immediately felt unworthy. How will I get there? How will I build the courage to be exposed in that capacity? The end-product is my development to that woman that walked confidently onto the platform because she knew her message would change lives. The process, the breaking, and the painful uproot is to birth a new me, one who accepts the reflection of His image in her own life. I cannot dim my own light to make others comfortable. I must move boldly toward the call because the next generation of messengers are watching.

~

The personal journey I began in September 2012 proved to be a life changing experience. If I knew then what I know now, I would say that's when I truly became a *God Chaser*. I decided that the dull, uneventful Sunday morning services were no longer enough. God could not be this boring and complacent.

After witnessing a woman named Kenya accepting Christ at my baptism in Nicaragua, I wanted more of that God, that powerful soul shaking experience. But, I couldn't find Him. That God didn't reside at the church I attended. I didn't know how to express that to my family members who sat beside me because they had no knowledge of the God I'd only recently met.

Without informing my family or fellow church members, I searched for that new God Monday thru Saturday and some Sunday evenings. Sunday mornings, I praised and worshipped with them none the wiser. My cousin and I attended various churches 7 days a week, sometimes twice in a day, searching and seeking for the majesty of God to appear. When I sing the song, "searched all over, couldn't find nobody, looked high and low, still couldn't find nobody", I mean that. I've lived and breathed that.

For months, I knocked church doors down to find where the living God resided. I was disappointed over and over. I left feeling still hungry for a true encounter and Word straight from the throne. Service after service, it was as if I was the only one that recognized that God was not there. I began to believe the church was dead.

Several months later, my cousin invited me to a church as a last effort before the New Year. Like Tommy Tenney, I knew I was on to something. It was there that I felt the God I'd encountered in Nicaragua again. I felt refreshed and restored from months of being starved and dehydrated in the spirit. I knew that I would eventually call this church home.

~

"We can be inside praying for Him to come while He passes by outside. Worse than that, the "insiders" miss Him while the "outsiders" march with Him!" – Tommy Tenney, *God Chasers*

I would hate to miss Him. There are so many preachers who intellectually know God's word but have little to no revelation. So many profess who God is, but how many of us really know Him? How many of us truly experience Him? Lately, I have been invited to events and engagements with people I thought were in love with God. I thought they had true encounters with Him.

Truth is, I was fooled, but not anymore. My experiences brought me to re-evaluate where I am now and where I am going. I have been so stuck in the past that I have missed the full effect of many moments by not being in the present. As a minister, I don't want to be like the political preachers and people-pleasing preachers. I want to know God for myself.

I remember when I would visit in church and the people didn't wait on the pastor to get there or to catch wind that she was on her way to get started. I remember how intercessory prayer at the beginning of service was intimate and had a burning fire to it. I remember when we were ushered into worship and prepared for an impartation, a meaty word and to meet God in a new way. Every service was unique and new.

I remember we would war cry for at least fifteen minutes and my pastor would say, "Let's go to war". Then, I would hear, "let's go higher church, let's go higher." I loved that, but now, I want more. Yes, I want to go higher, but we must get on one accord. I'm realizing that not everyone wants to go higher. I want to go so high that no man or circumstance can break my concentration on God when I come back down.

One of the worst things I've done to hinder my elevation in God is stopping to think too long and not seeking. My logic became my guide while God was my rebound if logic didn't work. My mind took me to my past and I didn't know how to get back to the present so that I could move forward.

The blessing of this burden is that I can better recognize when others are allowing their minds to hinder them as well. Thinking is not bad, but we must know and understand that *our* thoughts are not *the Lord's* thoughts. So many times, we have a specific idea of how we expect God to show up, but we are still getting to know Him.

Just like everyone has a different and separate deliverance, so it is with each visitation experience with God. It is amazing how many church buildings there are, but the number of people experiencing God's presence is low in comparison. There is a select group of people, a remnant, who can hear His voice and see Him move while others around are reaching without grasping, or too content in their current situation to reach at all.

One of our prime responsibilities is to be open and sensitive to His spirit. Tommy Tenney said it best - "It's time that we punch a hole in the Heavens and break through in hungry travail so that the Glory of God can begin to shine down on our city."

Anointing

The primary purpose of the anointing is to "camouflage the stench of our flesh"[1]. This does not mean to excuse our wrong as being good, but to allow us to remain in the graces of the King. Tommy Tenney states, "The real purpose of the anointing is not to make us sound good, look good, or smell good to man. That happens as a by-product, but the real purpose of the anointing is to give us favor in the King's chamber." Through this statement, I learned how the anointing covers our past faults and keeps us available to operate in the name of the Lord.

Many times, fear creeps in when you know there is a past, reputation, or scandal attached to your name and you do not know how it will affect your journey. Before we began to chase God, we had a life where many foolish decisions were made, and shameful actions took place that we cannot erase. During our chase, there are still unholy moments taking place until we catch Him. However, God always deserves the Glory in any and every situation or circumstance. God chose to like me when He put His anointing on me and my choice is to glorify Him with it, even when I feel unworthy.

With the anointing, repentance is very important. The anointing grants us His favor but our repentance grants us access to anywhere He is present, which is everywhere. Tenney writes, "We can brag on our accomplishments or our inadequacies but no matter what we do, only repentance will get us anywhere with God." A repentant heart will remain free and hungry for the Lord. There are no worries because you are free from dwelling on the past, free from fear of tomorrow, and free from being inadequate.

We are being made whole in the Lord; so, the freer and hungrier we are for Him, the more He will pour Himself into us. Acts 17:28 states, "In Him we live, we move, and we have our being". But, when we are consumed by our flesh we are choosing to not be with Him. Every time we choose our flesh, we must repent to get back in His present favor. There is more to Him than what He has shown today, but we can't access it with a stubborn and unrepentant heart or settling with a certain level of anointing.

---

[1] Tommy Tenney, *God Chasers*

Fulfill the requirements of the anointing you are blessed with, and He will give you more so that you can do more and handle more for Him.

Prayer

During prayer one night in Ministerial Training, I received a message. *If we are courageous enough to risk hurt, we can teach each other how to love. We can break traditions in the church of surface love with our fellow worshippers.*

I am done with surface level interaction, conversation, and communication. If we can't love each other for real, what's the point of it all? As our thirst and hunger for God grows, so will our desire for authentic relationships.

Church hurt steals trust. It ruptures the fundamentals of relationship building and inhibits us from a genuine love in a relationship of any capacity. So many of us complain about the lack of authenticity in our connections with fellow church members. We can quickly identify who doesn't value us or who we can't depend on, but can we be bold enough to be the *example* of love?

Prayer can reveal needed messages like this one to us if we practice it regularly. It is then our responsibility to act on what has been revealed to us. Here is a prayer that you can say to begin opening your spirit to receiving new truths.

Lord, open my ears of to your voice and peel the scales from my eyes to see your truth. Touch my heart with wisdom and understanding. In Jesus name, Amen.

~

Key tools we must possess are humility during prayer and the ability to be promoted by it are increased faith, endurance to handle the pain at the promotion, increased wisdom to endure the afflictions that ensure productivity, and a surrendered vessel in which to glorify God at all times.

Ask God as we move forward, *Lord, gird me up with strength, change the perception of what I see. Awake those sleeping areas within me that I need to press forward. Bring forth truth and holy discernment in this hour. Give me new armor to fight the new fight. Polish the weapons of my warfare and give me the posture of a soldier. Bring light to the darkness and relief to my weariness.*

Fasting

"I have compassion for these people; they have already been with me three days and have nothing to eat. If I send them home hungry, they will collapse on the way, because some of them have come a long distance."
- Mark 8:2-3, on Jesus feeding the multitude

Fasting is not only a way to stand in solidarity with those who are not able to eat daily, it clears the mind and the spirit and opens the gates to personal breakthroughs. Recently during a fast, I meditated on the scripture, Isaiah 43:19 (NIV): "For I am about to do something new. See, I have already begun! Do you not see it? I will make a pathway through the wilderness. I will create rivers in the dry wasteland." I needed this reminder because as my fast progressed, my life still did not seem to be aligned with what I've been promised. God's ways are not our ways, so we may not immediately see our breakthrough with our natural eyes while fasting and praying. We must have faith and remember His promise to use wilderness to create an avenue for a new thing.

This does not just mean that we must cross the wilderness to our destination. If this was the case, we would want to petition God to hurry us through the difficult parts of life and praise Him when we are comfortable again. We must remember that many times, we are being molded and strengthened through the hardships themselves. Just as our faith is tested by fire as presented in Peter 1:7, our characters are strengthened by the fire so that we can be the women and men of God that He intends for us to be.

Therefore, we must be grateful for the process. We must be honored that God loves us enough to push us to our best. When we fast, we do not escape the difficulties, but we can better understand and endure how they are shaping us. At times, clarity comes through prayer. Other times, our dreams reveal how God is working in our lives. In either case, we must pay attention to what we receive and act on it appropriately.

In my personal experience, God seems to speak louder during a fast or maybe my ears are more in tune to His voice and my eyes more open to His presence. For example, during a fast, I had a dream about female co-worker who was known for neglecting her children to party and boldly cheating on her husband. I was not sure about the meaning of the dream until speaking with my pastor about it. Through our conversation, I could recognize that I had been judging my co-worker about her choices without acknowledging that God was in her too. I began to see that she was not evil, but a survivor and hard worker who was trying to drink and party away pain she accumulated over the years. Though I tried to put it out of my mind, I also know what it's like to be dead on the inside, to suffer in silence, and to find comfort in the bottom of a pint. It is important that we do not forget our journey and judge others based on mistakes we've also made in the past. Compassion is key. Instead of seeing ourselves as saints and others as sinners, we can authentically pray for their breakthroughs. We can pray that God touch their broken places and release them from their pain.

Jesus fed the multitude because they were hungry, and in our fasting, we can go hungry to 'feed' the multitude. Not that we are feeding them physically, but learning to truly practice feeding others spiritually through first purifying our own lives.

How to Fast:
You can choose to abstain from one meal and spend that time in prayer or worship instead as a start. You could also choose one day per week to only drink water. If you want to engage in a deeper fast, you can drink only water for 1 – 7 days. Be sure to eat light (fruits and/or salads) in the days before and after your fast so that the process is not too hard on your body. Spend the time during your fast reading scripture, praying, praising, and listening for guidance.

Be sure to remember to take your prescribed medications during your fast and do not fast from food for full days if your medication(s) must be taken with food. These statements have not been approved by the FDA and we are not medical doctors. Be sure to consult with your doctor if you have health issues before, during, and/or after fasting.

Vulnerability

I will never forget what came from my mouth one day during a fervent prayer, "Lord, I'll do whatever to be found worthy". The revelation I received in my cup is vulnerability. I must bring my broken pieces to be considered for the assignment. It proves my worthiness to be made whole through him if I accept the challenge of vulnerability.

This is what true vulnerability feels like with my Father - surrender. It is uncomfortable and can be painful as so many times we like to feel that we are in full control. Our need for control brings us to run into relationships, new career positions, or pleasures trying to fulfill voids that can only be filled by God. This morning, God told me to stop running. I replied, "Father, I'm here, I'm engaged in the process." I repented for trying to do it on my own and surrendered to the Lord.

It is not only important to be vulnerable with God, willing to humble ourselves, willing to go where He wants us to go, but to be vulnerable in our relationships with others. I have faulted God for my misjudgment of being vulnerable with people that were not worthy. For example, if we see friends, family members or coworkers living their lives outside of what has been prescribed by scripture, it is easy to get on our high horses and feel that we are better than them. We can go to lunch after church and talk about all that they are doing wrong and why they don't seek God. Or, we can be vulnerable enough to remember when we too lived lives that did not glorify God. We can use this vulnerability to have compassion for others instead of judging them.

~

After my surrender into vulnerability, I felt shipwrecked. My surroundings felt unfamiliar and my exact location felt unknown. I feared I would not be rescued because my ship would come up on no one's radar. Instead of trying to salvage what I could from the wreckage, I had to allow God to remake me, starting with remaking my heart.

I knew the journey ahead would be long, difficult, and lonely as I walked in a completely new territory in the spirit. I felt unworthy and uncomfortable. However, with closed eyes, I saw acceleration and promotion. There was a small aircraft flying through a dark tunnel. It suddenly inclined and hit rays of light. I knew that no matter how arduous my journey, God was delivering me to brighter days walking in His will.

When God told me to stop running, it meant for me to allow him to fix me, allow Him to fill my voids. I tried to fix myself in the past with accomplishments, inebriants, sex, and even self-loathing – but, God's fixes are permanent. God not only heals, but makes my scabs fall away and scars fade.

Before my surrender, I could no longer see the real me. She was buried beneath layers of self-doubt and disbelief. I did not even know where to look. When I disassociated from my true self, a willing servant of God, it seemed only my fake self survived. My fake self made great public appearances and was admired by others. She excelled at work. Her hair and makeup was always perfect and she easily attracted men. She showed up at church on Sundays after staying out until all hours with friends on Saturday nights.

As I drew closer to God, I recognized the self I thought was real was a fragment of who others told me I was. There is no real me until I draw to Him. He defines and molds me. The true me is a reflection of Him.

How do we learn to be vulnerable when we are taught to simply project an image of success? How do we learn to be vulnerable again when we have been trained to be closed, unreachable, and un-penetrable? How does who we are in the flesh hinder who we are in the spiritual?

To be watchmen in the Kingdom, we must practice surrender first, and then self-control and discipline to watch our thoughts. Our thoughts lead to our actions and then our habits. It is so much harder for us to hear from God if our thoughts control us. Our thoughts of what we desire, of how these desires will make us feel temporarily, and of how others expect us to be, including our long-time friends.

Through controlling our thoughts, we can attain free, uninterrupted communication with God. This does not mean that thoughts do not enter our minds that are not of God. Yet, when these thoughts come, we rebuke them and recall who God is shaping us to be and what He is calling us to do.

Habakkuk 2:1 states, "I will climb my watchtower and wait to see what the Lord will tell me to say and what answer He will give to my complaint." Our daily watchtowers are our minds. In a watchtower, you are looking out to see when the enemy approaches. They cannot take you by surprise because you are up high and they are down low. Consider your thoughts this way. As you see thoughts approaching that could take you outside of God's will, do not surrender to them; surrender to God and rebuke them.

Exes that I have sinned with have tried to come back into my life as temptations. The enemy will play mind games when you know you are in good relationship with God. When we are also having challenges in our personal lives, temporary pleasures can seem to be band-aids that would take our minds away from daily struggles with work, family, and finances.

It's easy to feel like God can only accept our light, and to try to go outside of Him to release our darkness. Our darkness feels safe drinking with friends or having empty sex. When our motivation and inspiration is gone, it can feel so hard to get on our knees and give it all to God. We do not even feel worthy.

That is the time when it is most important to trust our darkness with God too. Instead of running away to temptation, confide in Him and let Him know how we are struggling. He won't see us as weak. He doesn't view us as ungrateful. He won't push us away. He will embrace us, strengthen us, and give us the guidance we need.

Perseverance

Job 27 teaches us about perseverance. When we are engaging in daily prayer, consistent fasting, and surrender to God, it is not an easy or automatic journey. There are times we will feel glorious and other times when we experience a rollercoaster of emotions.

Reflecting on Job 27, we can recall not only the struggles Job faced but his ability to stand firm and not allow others to declare who he was. I aspire to someday have this trust in who God says that I am and in the integrity in my heart to not waver or profess that I achieved only through my own abilities. I am closer than I have ever been, but I understand I have a lot of growing up to do.

Job understood that without God he was nothing, a mere nobody. He trusted God's sovereignty and recognized the authority of his creator. My questions when reading were, when did Job learn of God's sovereignty and how did he come to believe so strongly?

I found that he has always known, but in this chapter of his life he gained a deeper understanding. At this point, the truth he has always believed in and lived by was being embedded in his members. He was down to his final words of I am who God says that I am, and God is the only one who can change that.

We are taught not to question authority, but we all desire understanding. Inquiring of the Lord is how we get to know Him and not fall for foolery. When we lack understanding or resources leading to understanding, we tend to create value in our own foolish solutions and opinions like Job's friends. We are naturally an impatient body of people.

Job begins with his exhortation of how mighty and sovereign the Lord is. He expounds on the majesty of the Lord's decisions and how he would stand firm in who he is until the day of his death. He lists out the consequences of the wicked; he has experienced them all. It makes sense to speak of the Lord's sovereignty, but when you have done your best to remain upright how you do accept experiencing the consequences of the wicked? How do you decipher between the being one of the considered and one of the wicked?

In verses 7 - 9, I found that the wicked are identified by their lack of hope which causes them to continuously stray away from doing what is right. Verse 8 states, "For what hope have the Godless when they are cut off, when God takes away their life?" At least the Godly have the hope in the future during times of distress; hope that one day, all will be well. I learned that it is our hope that separates us. Faith, hope, and love abide!

Job's focus was on remaining just and righteous despite the unimaginable hardships. Verses 2 – 4 of Job 27 state, "As surely as God lives, who has denied me justice, the Almighty, who has made my life bitter, as long as I have life within me the breath of God in my nostrils, my lips will not say anything wicked, and my tongue will not utter lies." No matter the situation, circumstance or uncertainty, remember it is the Lord that gives and the Lord that takes away. I've heard it, I've said it, and I've read it, but now, I get it. We are only owners by inheritance.

God has been taking me through a stripping process for the past year or so. There is a major difference in being stripped and being pruned. To be pruned is to be made fruitful by removing the dead portions, but to be stripped is to have everything taken away. Before this stripping, I felt comfortable giving up habits, material goods, and people because I willingly obeyed and yielded to the pruning. I knew the pruning was for my own good. But then, things began taking place that I didn't understand, and God wasn't explaining (or I didn't want to hear the truth).

Job was identified as being blameless and full of integrity, yet who would have ever imagined the Lord would permit him to go through all that he went through? He experienced the snatching of his earthly worth and the identity the world knew him by. I believe Job was considered not just because he could handle it, but because there was greater in him than the greatness he had already achieved. We can become too comfortable in our accomplishments.

Job was wiped clean and restored with double. His territory and capacity to receive and give were expanded in a way that wouldn't have taken place without this encounter with God. In my own struggles, only God knows my faults thoroughly and how I need to be made over, but no matter how challenging life becomes for me, I know I love God and He loves me. I know he wants the best for me. I know he hears my cries. I know that even when all looks like it's failing, and no answer is given, He is in control. I trust both the pruning and the stripping processes because I am honored to allow God to be greater within me.

Deliverance

To remain free during our purging process, we must continually rededicate ourselves to Christ. As more of those buried toxins surface, we cannot dwell on memories, but must immediately place them in our Father's hands. Discipline during this process will ensure our peace.

During my personal purging journey, I experience some of the deepest, darkest valleys I've ever encountered. As God drew the impurities from my well and removed the toxins which contributed to my spiritual sickness, I thought I would surely die. As I continued to seek and chase Him, I was reminded of those miserable moments. Yet, I also recalled how He saved me. Even when I fell into pits where no one else could see me, there He stood. He never left my side.

In the scripture, the Samaritan woman at the well was offered living water by Jesus. Meditating on this, I wondered why he offered her living water and not well water. I recalled how I could not drink from wells at schools I visited to volunteer in Ghana, West Africa, because the impurities were foreign to my body and would make me sick. Jesus did not dwell on the woman's past or offer her water that would have negative effects on her body; he offered her living water to give her everlasting life. It quenched her thirst to the point where she offered it to others, even those naysayers who were fixated on her past.

Jesus loved her unconditionally and she practiced unconditional love by releasing attachment to her past and forgiving those who had judged her. This process had been a struggle for me – loving unconditionally. For many years, my tongue was my tool, my sharpened weapon I utilized in the daily battles I came against with any and everyone because everyone was an enemy. This behavior, habit, and mastered skill required a daily death to unlearn it. Anyone with an archived knowledge capable to hurt me was a potential threat and target.

Then, God showed me a vision of myself with a muzzle on my mouth. I heard a word in my mind that had become a foreign character trait to me - meekness. Since it was so difficult for me to truly practice love towards everyone, I struggled to follow this vision and master silence when I wanted to speak non-constructively.

With this new quietness, some of my peers felt I was uninterested or even ignorant. For so long, I fought to be heard, to be right, and to be louder than the negative voice in my head. God led me to relearn the art of silence, reclaim the essence of silence in my heart and my mind.

In this silence, I realized that it was so difficult for me to practice unconditional love towards others because of all the pain that still lived within me. I felt others were unworthy of my love because of all the pain that I had not allowed to heal and all the people who I had not truly forgiven. I had been spiritually molested by men I thought were my spiritual fathers. My pain had been ignored by spiritual mothers who did not want to call out these injustices. There was an invisible paralysis that plagued me from all the hurt I had left unspoken that manifested as a verbal bitterness towards others.

If we are not actively allowing ourselves to be emptied, we will not see the root of what blocks us from the next step in our journey. If we are not empty, there is no room for God to fill us. Secrets we hold inside make us sick and take up space where God is attempting to dwell. If my body is a temple and my temple is crowded with rotting hurts, nothing new can reside in me. My freedom lives in a free space within me.

Spiritually, what we have not given to God to heal slows our life's progresses like a traffic jam. We can stop and go, slowly, but there are repeated delays. Once we clear what is hindering us by facing it and giving it to God, we are free to move forward. We are freed from bondage, chaos, and worry into the freedom of worthiness, sound mind, and true worship. We are birthed anew.

A Covenant

While reading chapter one of The Covenant, the first point standing out to me was the word covenant means "to cut". This immediately took me to separation. When God does a new thing, it calls for separation to take place. It is separation from the lies, old beliefs and thoughts. On page 12, he said, "it was as if scales fell off my eyes." Though he was referring to the speaker's revelations removing the scales from his eyes, I believe this is the same with entering in a covenant of ministry. Once in the ministry, scales began to be removed from your eyes. A covenant is a new beginning because you are letting go of some things and gaining new things. Now you have to become accustomed to this new way of life and own what you have taken on.

Second, Mr. Garlow states, "By making a covenant with humanity, God would bind himself to them and ask them to bind themselves to Him." The following quote is a great spark for the common prayer: I want less of me and more of you, Lord. We must leave behind what formerly identified who we are and become one (whole) in God. The Bible gives many directives to giving God all or nothing. For example, Revelation 3:15-17 "'I know your works: you are neither cold nor hot. Would that you were either cold or hot! 16 So, because you are lukewarm, and neither hot nor cold, I will spit you out of my mouth. 17 For you say, I am rich, I have prospered, and I need nothing, not realizing that you are wretched, pitiable, poor, blind, and naked." I chose this scripture to show when entering covenant with God we have an obligation to be obedient to His commands and when we are not there are repercussions. It is important to not become caught up in the physical blessings but remember the entirety of the covenant. God has His part and we have ours, which is obedience.

Restoration

St. John 4 is a blessing. I have always wondered the depths of worshiping God in Spirit and in truth. Intellectually, I knew to come to Him wholeheartedly but there was a barrier in my understanding. This barrier was the fact that, I hadn't reached or accepted that truth in myself. Often, I would let others dictate who I am supposed to be and tell me what does and does not make sense.

When the woman at the well replied to Jesus that she had no husband He said, "18 For thou hast had five husbands; and he whom thou now hast is not thy husband: in that saidst thou truly." (KJV). Jesus enlightens this woman about spiritual renewal and then asked the right question to have her set free. Because her truth was revealed, she was free from shame and guilt and open to testify about his greatness.

Verse 11 reminds me of one of my favorite scriptures, Psalms 42:7: "Deep calls to deep in the roar of your waterfalls; all your waves and breakers have swept over me." (NIV). The word deep in this text is a surging mass of water or an abyss. When the woman at the well asked Jesus, "The well is too deep, what will you draw with?", there was a tension foreshadowing that she would never be restored with hope and a future. However, the troubles of her soul that enticed her to act immorally would indeed fade from her care into the hands of our Redeemer. Jesus states, "But whosoever drinketh of the water that I shall give him shall never thirst; but the water that I shall give him shall be in him a well of water springing up into everlasting life." (KJV).

Living water is eternal or everlasting life. The well of eternal life is in us, so when troubles come, the waters will surge from within us to remind God's children of who we are and what we live for. The waters will help us to not thirst for the satisfaction of this world, but be satisfied in Him who created us. Lord, remind us of the big picture. Keep your children in line with your will and focused on your love. I pray we stay close to You and abide in You as You abide in us. Help us to live justly, love mercifully, and walk humbly. Teach us to come to You in spirit and in truth. In Jesus name I pray, Amen.

A 21-Day Journey to Restoration Devotional

Day 1: Confess Your Faith

Confess your faith to the Lord. You can begin with:
I believe that I have an intimate, personal relationship with my Father.
I am chosen by Him to make a tangible impact in the Kingdom.
By faith, I am moving closer and closer daily to reaching my full potential.
I believe in His power to rescue me from the deepest pits and the lowest valleys.
I am a daughter/son to the Most High King.
By faith, I am only led by the Holy Spirit.
I believe He is the steward over my life in each and every area.
I am the head and not the tail.
By faith, I am healed of every invisible paralysis.
I believe my mind is covered and shielded by God.
I am an overcomer.
In Jesus name, Amen.

There is power in "I am" statements. "I am" is a substitute for God in a sentence; therefore, when we say, "I am", whatever follows is speaking to the God in us. There is power in our words, freedom in our voices.

Your later shall be your greater and your later is now. There are no weapons formed or forming against you that will prosper because all things are already working together for your good. As you press forward, know that you are who God says you are! Rejoice and be glad in it. You are esteemed and strengthened in the Lord Almighty. You are a blessing to others.

You can abide in the Lord by abiding in faith, hope, and love. You can shift minds, break traditions, and change generational patterns in your family and community. You will achieve this through choosing your thoughts and ways to be as the Lord's. Mountains will move, seas will part, demons will tremble, and souls will be won into the Kingdom through your obedience.

Day 2: Accept the Past

Therapy patients often complete an exercise where they replay events that happened in the past that caused them pain or trauma and reflect on how those feelings reappear in their lives presently. In my personal life, I recognized that I was still holding on to fears from situations that occurred during my childhood. In those moments, I lost my sense of security and felt that trusting someone completely to take care of me was out of the question.

Though I am longer a child, these feelings still live within me. For a time, they hindered me from completely trusting God. Take time to reflect on times in your life when you felt most abandoned or hurt. Write down your thoughts or talk about them with a trusted friend to release them from your heart. Ask God to heal the broken places and wounds that left you feeling you could never fully depend on others. If you need to, write letters to those who have hurt you telling them how you feel, and then allow yourself to forgive them and throw these letters away.

Pray, "God I accept that my past is behind me and ask you to clean the wounds that still haunt me. I asked that you heal me completely and thoroughly. Please help me to embrace You and trust You in the present to guide my life. You are not a man that you should lie. You will never leave me or forsake me. Release me of any emotions that would prevent me from surrendering to You and Your will fully. In Jesus name, Amen."

Day 3: Practicing Faith

Job 27 is a powerful representation of why Job is blameless and integral. What I love about Job is that he says to the people that witness his loss his grief that *God is still good*. What measure of faith Job had in God! He truly respected and accepted the supremacy and sovereignty of God.

In verses 7-10, Job teaches the doubters how much better off he is than they are. The man who has lost everything, who has seemingly been cursed by God and has nothing left but his breath and his sanity, preaches to the unbelievers why he continues to trust in God. Job explains that even in his misery, he still has the luxury and privilege to call on his Father. Regardless of circumstance, Job declares that his Father listens, and the doubters do not have access to that relationship.

Can we practice faith this deeply? When everything in our life seems to be going wrong on a material level, can we rejoice because we still have the most priceless possession of all, a relationship with God? Verse 10 of Job 27 states, "can they take delight in the Almighty?" Job reveals that even in his trial, he still delights in God. He reiterates, "Can they call to God at any time?" In the midst of hell on Earth, he seeks the ear of the Almighty not to complain, but because he is yet believing for restoration. While it is not an easy feat, we must seek to practice this level of faith in our lives.

We can practice faith through expressing gratitude for God's grace and mercy no matter how things may seem. We must recall that our faith is not a magic key to receiving "double" what we had before, but a testament of our love and reverence for God. We may not always find that our blessings in the material realm double. We may lose a high paying job and take a job with lower pay or status to support our families. This does not mean that God has shorted us or failed us. We may learn lessons that will benefit our spirit through our new position. We may simplify our lives and place less value on materialism. Our bond with our family may grow stronger. We may minister to someone from this new position. We don't get to choose *how* God is blessing us based on what we think we should receive. It is our job to simply have faith, no matter the circumstance, with the objective being our relationship with God being strengthened.

Day 4: Embracing God's Strength

God sent me to Judges 6 for a Gideon impartation - if God sends you, He sends you with *His* strength (verse 14). I knew Gideon was the least of his family, but I didn't realize Gideon was the least of the weakest clan. When the Lord called him, before Gideon answered, The Lord named him a "mighty hero". We may not be the most qualified or experienced persons at our jobs, the most respected in our families, or the most accomplished in our communities – but when God calls us to a position, it is His to assign.

We may worry that we are not enough when God opens the door for us to step to higher greatness, but it is His will, not ours. God hears our worrying and doubting and encourages us to let go and let Him work through us. We must truly, "Let go and let God!"

When we think we are not good enough, we will find that God possesses all goodness. When we think we can do it on our own, we will find great feats impossible. When we let go and allow God to strengthen us, to open doors for us, and to make all things possible, we will find that no mountain is too massive to move!

This does not always mean we will achieve what we thought we would achieve in life. Perhaps our desires are fueled by what others want us to be, selfishness, or materialism. God needs people who are willing to give up their hopes, dreams, visions, and desires for their lives and live for His people and His purposes. This may not look like missionary or ministerial work – God may place you in a certain position with your family or with your job to be an example of His love.

As we align ourselves with God's will, we will see that our dreams are aligned with God's dreams for us. When this happens, you will say, wow, my dreams are all coming true. Your dreams have been conformed to match the Father's. At this point, your dreams are no longer about you, but about surrendering to and living according to His will!

Prayer: "Father, help me to release the fear and let you re-shape my life and my desires. Shake me and remove what is not of you. Take my heavy thoughts, restore my spirit, strengthen me and allow me to serve you as you wish. Thank you! In Jesus name, Amen."

Day 5: Perspective

On page 27 of *God Chasers*, Tenney stated that God told him, " Son, if they were physically starving, they would act differently." I understand this revelation because starving people have taught me life changing lessons and transformed my worldview. While in Ghana, I gained a frame of reference of how people with nothing could have so much more than I.

I did not know what true contentment looked like or genuine gratefulness or a real respect for provision. In Nicaragua, I saw the same starvation and the same gratitude. It was as if God had transported the poverty surroundings from Africa, implanted them in Nicaragua and changed the skin color and language of the people. If I looked at the scenery alone, I could be either in Ghana or Nicaragua.

The lesson God taught me, most importantly, is that where I live doesn't look like either of those places, the people I'm around are well-fed and educated, but we lack true gratitude for the blessings others go without daily.

If the church were physically starving, we would have the positive attitude and outlook of a Nicaraguan, the faith and thirst for God of a Ghanaian, the peace of a people starving physically but full spiritually. Instead, we settle for what Tenney calls, "a residue of fading glory", too sluggish physically and spiritually to chase after more.

We must allow our flesh to continue to tremble in His presence. We must allow ourselves to be continually overwhelmed with gratitude for His sacrifice. How can we ever repay Him? We do not have to be perfect, but we can aim for perfect praise and worship. We can practice humility and thankfulness daily, gratitude for God's mercy, no matter how we experience life's ups and downs.

Day 6: Love

Love is another form of worship. As we go higher, know and experience Him more, the deeper our worship goes. This is the same with love. I have hurt many for the sake of trying not to be hurt anymore, but that is not my position or purpose. If I love my enemies, then I love what hurts me.

Last week I learned this powerful lesson – love causes us to receive pain at times, but through that pain, peace is produced. I can hear confusion waiting outside the door for the moment when doubt creeps in, so I must be as mindful of the Father as He is of me. I must remember to always think, act, and live in love. Despite my many flaws, God loves me. I ask Him, "Who am I that you are mindful of me? Thank you, Father, for Love, Grace and Mercy! Perfect our love in Jesus name, Amen." If God can love us despite our shortcomings, and what a gift that is, then we can be strong enough to pass that gift on to others. The greatest gift is love! 1 Corinthians 13 teaches us how to love.

1 Corinthians 13:4 - 8 New International Version (NIV):

[4] Love is patient, love is kind. It does not envy, it does not boast, it is not proud. [5] It does not dishonor others, it is not self-seeking, it is not easily angered, it keeps no record of wrongs. [6] Love does not delight in evil but rejoices with the truth. [7] It always protects, always trusts, always hopes, always perseveres.

[8] Love never fails. But where there are prophecies, they will cease; where there are tongues, they will be stilled; where there is knowledge, it will pass away.

Day 7: Repentance

In repenting, after asking for forgiveness and expressing our desire to truly change, we can repeat the phrase, "I am absolutely nothing without God, Our Father and Lord." In these words, we step out of our ego and fully surrender. It is here that we can be sensitive to His Divine Will. This unraveling will not be easy or comfortable, nor do we want it to be. The art of staying broken becomes beautiful when we humble ourselves and transfer our will to His.

In 2 Chronicles 7:14 KJV, we read, "If my people, which are called by my name, shall humble themselves, and pray, and seek my face, and turn from their wicked ways; then will I hear from heaven, and will forgive their sin, and will heal their land." Humbling ourselves in repentance and truly submitting to God can be an ugly, all-night affair at times with a wet face and swollen nose. Fear of going this deeply can keep us on the surface with a simple, "Father, forgive me." Repentance is not only asking for forgiveness, it is truly recognizing our wrongs and giving them over to God. We are making a commitment in repentance to let His will be done in our lives. While it is hard, it will not kill us. It will only kill the parts of us that are holding us back from truly walking in His will.

While repentance is challenging, it is a necessary step. These is absolutely no possession, person, or setting that can satisfy our voids - only God. When we repent, we stay connected to Him through being desperate for a deeper connection. We release all that does not serve Him. We proclaim, "Forget who I use to be and help me be who you called me to be!"

Prayer: "Today my answer is, "Yes, Lord!" I repent for being impatient and fearful. I'm good at many things. but the one I say yes to is the one You want me to be great in and allow the others to help me in my elevations. My instructions are to keep my eyes on You and my ears listening for Your voice. Please remove all that does not serve you. Shape my thoughts, my actions, and my life to serve you. Shape my relationships and my career to serve you. I let go of my will and embrace Your will, Lord. Break me down and grow me anew that so I may be worthy! In Jesus name, Amen!"

Day 8: Obedience

Many of life's experiences for me have been difficult. I'm learning now to get to where God wants me to be. I have to press through the pressure. I had been spoiled. I had gotten used to and expected to have favor.

We can all be like this sometimes – feeling that our winning streaks are due to our own efforts and getting away from giving credit to the Lord. Then, when we do not seem to be winning anymore, we wonder why God is not hearing our call rather than asking ourselves, are we being receptive and obedient to His will?

When I became unappreciative and took favor for granted, God allowed me to see what life is like without His hands on it. When my job started to use me for God's will, I walked out because of my ego even though every word I received had been "do not move." I missed the blessing at the end of that journey and I was chastised for it. Afterwards, I was given the same opportunity in a similar job – helping others through submitting to God's will, but dealing with difficult people along the way. This time, I did not allow my ego to slow God's plan for me.

Remember that just like the oyster, our best is developed under pressure. When God calls us to a certain position or life circumstance, it is time to be obedient, not to run away because of fear or ego. If you are unsure if God wants you to go this way or that way, just ask. Then, be still and listen.

Pray, "Father, please give me clear guidance so I can follow Your will and not mine. Please lead me where You want me to go. Thank You for allowing me to serve You with my life. Thank You for loving me enough to lead me. In Jesus name, Amen."

Day 9: Sensitive to the Spirit

One day at work, the middle of the afternoon was interrupted by a teenager admitted for attempting to hang himself in a police car. When I sat down to assess him, he was in relatively good spirits after wrapping a seat belt around his neck. I could see the scar around his neck from how tight the seat belt had gotten. I asked him about the pain of coming so close to death and being unable to breathe. The cops had to cut the belt from around his neck. The explanation he gave me blew my mind.

He said that he prefers physical pain to the mental pain he endures every day. He said the escape he feels between the last breaths and death is worth the release from his daily Hell. I wonder how many people we meet daily, and even sitting in the pews of the church, have the same secret desire to escape life. Do we recognize this hurt in others? Do we see how they have given up hope?

The busy nature of daily lives and preoccupation with our own problems can desensitize us to the emotional state of even those closest to us. It is important to pray, fast, and read scripture often to ease our minds and calm our spirits so that we can see clearly. This will help us to keep our discernment, so we can see when someone around us is teetering on the edge of their sanity.

Pray, "Thank you, Lord, for a clear mind and calm spirit so that I can see clearly and walk without stumbling. In Jesus name, Amen."

Day 10: Leave Space for God

I have learned to steal away to be with my Father. Not necessarily my physical being leaving a room or the presence of others but connecting with Him no matter where I am. So, when people ask where my mind is, I chuckle or smile because sometimes I forget I left. This is how I keep my sanity.

God has had me in a quiet place where many times He wants me to just listen even when He's not speaking. I am growing in my knowledge and understanding of Him by enjoying him. What I could do better in my relationship with God is not allow others to make me miss or shorten my appointments with God.

We all need this time with the Father. In the middle of your busy day, in the center of your storm, take a minute to get quiet and listen. You may receive a message on your heart that will give you strength, reassurance, or guidance. You may not recognize anything at all, besides the stillness. Know that this in stillness, God's love is present. Even if you cannot quiet your mind and your thoughts are racing about this and that, remember Psalms 139. God's thoughts of you outnumber the grains of sand and His love for you is just as vast.

Psalms 139: 17 - 18

[17] How precious to me are your thoughts,[a] God!
    How vast is the sum of them!
[18] Were I to count them,
    they would outnumber the grains of sand—
    when I awake, I am still with you.

Day 11: Self-Examination

When I do not feel God, or I feel He is distant, I first do a self-examination. This is my time to meditate, listen, seek Him, and be obedient to my previous or current instructions. This is not always easy because it took much work to get here and I still have a long way to go in my discipline and consistency in trust. Reflecting on the cross and the walk of Jesus are vital. Jesus gave His life so that we could live. He gave it all so that we could have it all.

In your life, when you are feeling disconnected from God, take time to look within yourself. Is there some pain inside from a human that hurt you that you have not addressed? Is there something you need to forgive and release? Or maybe it's time to visit a new church and get refreshed.

Another option is to pray and then write down all the reasons you are grateful. While writing a gratitude list may sound cliché, it is highly effective. You can start with *Lord, I thank you for…* and then start your list. You may begin with *food, water, a warm bed,* and then specific blessings in your life.

The gratitude list is so effective because we often lose sight of how God is working in our lives in the moment because we are so far from where we want to be. We may see the job we do not have, the marriage we do not have or that is not where we want it to be, the money that is not adding up, and forget about how far God has brought us and the gifts of the spirit[2] we have gained along the way.

When we pray, we can also pray for gifts of the spirit. Ask God, "Lord, I want to live according to Your will and Your Word. Please help me cultivate love, joy, peace, forbearance, kindness, goodness, faithfulness, gentleness, and self-control in my heart and in my life. These gifts are what I desire most of all, more than any material possession or worldly acquisition. Please purify my heart so that I understand that even in the midst of trials, you are sowing these true gifts within me. In Jesus name, Amen."

---

[2] Galatians 5:22-23

Day 12: Thicker than Blood

Here is the truth that hurts, we can sometimes feel more of a need for our spiritual family than our natural family. The battle with our blood families can be harsh. Some of us have very loving families while others have families that are not supportive or understanding. We are taught to stand by our families no matter what and yes, we should always practice love. However, there is no shame in feeling closer to your spiritual family.

There is nothing like the feeling of being excited about Christ with those who are just as passionate. It is such a comfort to the heart to have a shoulder you can cry on and a hand to hold as you walk to the altar. This is not to say that you will feel closeness with everyone you attend church with, but you will feel a deep sense of family with some you meet on your walk with God. That is nothing to be ashamed of; it is wonderful! Remember Acts 2:44, "And all who believed were together had all things in common."

If your family does not want to hear you talk about scripture or wants you to relax a little and have a drink instead of being such a "holy roller", do not fret. Lean on your spiritual family. Get together for a Bible study over dinner. Pray together over the phone. Lean on God together. Blood may be thicker than water, but God is thicker than blood.

Day 13: Works in Progress

We can be so focused on our careers and on our personal problems that our focus shifts from Christ. Remember, Jesus did not strive for accomplishments, but to live as an example of love. This is not to say that we have to be perfect, or to spend our lives feeding the hungry and clothing the naked instead of pursuing our goal; but, in all that we do, we can be works in progress to walk like Christ.

In our day jobs, we can let the light of Christ shine through. In our families, with our friends, in the grocery store, on the phone with the bill collectors, with a stranger who cut us off in traffic, we can allow Christ to shine through us.

On our worst days, we can lean on Him in prayer and worship. On our best days, we can strive to give Him the glory instead of crediting ourselves. Keep in mind that though we were not created as perfect people, we were created to be perfected by God. Pray that He keeps you focused to be a work in progress.

Day 14: Staying Focused

We all have problems and we all have baggage that won't fit through the narrow gate. Our challenge is not to somehow be so holy that we are above having problems, whether they be external or internal, but to stay focused on God in the process.

Even when obstacles vex us or the past haunts us, it is our duty to give it to God. It is our job to trust and obey. It is our mission to ask Him, "God, what are You teaching me from this situation? What would You have me to do next?" Not every stumbling block is meant to trip us; some are meant to be stepping stones for us to rise to our new station in Christ.

It's easy to feel frustrated when life seems out of your control. It's easy to feel that we are all alone, that no one is in our corner. So many of us slip into fear, anger, or depression more often than we would like to admit. Stay focused on the Lord.

Pray, "God, this is a lifelong process and I cannot do it in my own strength or knowledge. LORD, conform me into your image and help me to desire more faith, more hope, and more love. In Jesus name, Amen."

Day 15: Get Out There

Jesus had a heart not only for his parents or his disciples, but for the whole world. How can we love the world if we never get out there? Don't limit yourself to your city for outreach, take a mission trip when you can. Visit one of the many countries of Africa or Central America and see how others in the world are praising God.

Our thinking can be local, global, *and* eternal. Our mission is not just about our home or our church, but the world. The first step is simply to get your passport. It may take some time to save up or fundraise to take your first mission trip, but it will be so worth it.

Step 1: Take a passport photo. This can usually be done at your local pharmacy or post office.

Step 2: Apply for a passport. Check travel.state.gov for your options. You may need to purchase your ticket first for certain return speeds.

Step 3: Decide which organization or church that you will be traveling with, when, and where.

Step 4: Complete the registration steps with the organization or church.

Step 5: Get your passport ready, pack up, and go serve!

Some mission trips may require you to pay a fee. You can fundraise or save money from your income to prepare for the costs. Remember, the experience of serving those in need as a representative of Christ will be priceless! Get out there!

Day 16: Facing Our Fears

Fears of inadequacy and failure can hinder us. What if no one wants to hear what we have to say? What if our weaknesses are not only exposed but also highlighted? To avoid the spotlight and risk of failing, we may hide or shut down.

We must trust God enough to completely let go, to shed the aesthetic misconception of confidence and allow Him to move freely. We cannot maintain full control of our lives and surrender completely to His will. If we are focused on the external, we will see how God is moving in others, but not in ourselves.

Write out the answers to the following questions in your journal or discuss with a trusted friend.

1. What do you feel called to do at your greatest?
2. What are your fears about serving your full purpose in Christ?
3. What areas of your personality or life lead you to feel 'not good enough'?
4. What are your strengths?
5. What are 10 great things your closest friends or family would say about you?

Now that you have identified your fears and perceived inadequacies, as well as your strengths, it's time to push through those fears and focus on your strengths. What we focus on grows in our mind. What we feed grows in our lives. God would not give you a vision unless you can fulfill it.

If you are still unsure about your purpose, think of what you are good at. Take baby steps to shine in your strengths. Continue praying and serving and over time, your purpose will come to you. Even if you feel afraid, live in it boldly, step by step, every day.

Day 17: In the Darkness

At times, life will leave us drowsy and weak, lacking energy, enthusiasm, and motivation. We can feel this way not only physically, but spiritually. It is during these times that we must not give in to the brokenness, but give it over to God to be made whole.

This will not always be an immediate or overnight process. The darkness may feel like it will never leave, especially when we feel we have given all we have to give, are heartbroken, or are experiencing grief. It is then that we must stay on the path and pray, "God, revive me. Rekindle my light that is flickering and threatening to die. I need You to refuel me. Energize my body and quench my spirit. Reawaken my thirst for life and my thirst for You. I know that even in the darkness, you have promised me brighter days. I trust you and I know that this too, shall pass. In Jesus name, Amen."

Day 18: Family in Christ

Fellowship in the church has always been a bittersweet experience for me. Just as believers can offer God false worship, we engage in false fellowship with our sisters and brothers. Living a life that is not authentic, sharing bits and pieces of ourselves that we permit people to know, camouflaging the inconsistencies in our lives that keep us bound are ways that we hinder fellowship.

Do you develop true friendships with those in your church? Do you seek to understand as much as you seek to be understood? Do you give help when it is asked of you and ask for help when you need it? Do you have sisters or brothers in your church that you would trust with your deepest secrets or your life? If not, it is time to develop those relationships. If you truly feel that you cannot develop them within your current church group, then it may be time to start visiting new churches to find your home.

Church is meant to not only be a place for us to fulfill our duty and feel revived, but to find fellowship with those who we trust and love. Many churches are suffering from gossip and false relationships. This is not the fault of the church, but the people within it who are afraid to be authentic. It is up to you to be change that you want to see. By being the change, you can inspire others to open up as well.

Are you afraid of being hurt if you reveal yourself to others? Are you afraid that they will not like or love the real you? Your heart cannot truly be broken, though you can feel deep disappointment. Christ can heal this hurt. Take those risks – the rewards will be greater than any hurts you may experience along the way to joining or creating a group with which you can truly fellowship.

Day 19: When No One's Watching

I remember hearing on a Valentine's Day conference call, "In the Promised Land, Check Your Level of Integrity," and not fully understanding what that meant. God has dealt with me about character this entire year and I am beginning to understand why at the end. I have been in some
high places with low integrity. God allowed me to perform on a world stage with little perception of the importance of integrity. I simply had never been taught the dangers of operating without integrity.

The revolving doors of starting over in seemingly same cycles are because my level of integrity had not increased to an acceptable place for Him. When I fell to low places, the only way I could climb out is through heightened integrity.

Integrity does not only mean doing the right thing when no one is watching. Integrity means watching our thoughts, our conversations, our prayer habits, our fasting habits, our Bible study habits, and of course, the way that we treat others. Are we in traffic cursing out the driver who cut us off? Check yourself. Repent and reset your heart to love. Are we holding on to resentment towards those who have hurt us? Repent and reset your heart to love.

Resetting our hearts to love may seem like a difficult or even impossible feat. When we feel this challenge in our hearts, it is time to call on God. We can go deeper into our prayer and ask that all blockages be removed from loving as Jesus loved.

To change our mindset to one of integrity, we can also practice acting out of love and righteousness. Feed the homeless, volunteer, serve in your church – each of these actions will sow integrity in your heart. Practice loving those who are most difficult to love. For example, if there is someone who you have a really strained relationship with, write down ten things about them that you authentically appreciate or admire. Do this for each person that you feel has wronged you or who you simply don't like. This will help you to see the good in them and consequently, to treat them with more authentic love.

Day 20: Releasing Entitlement

"It is for freedom that Christ has set us free. Stand firm, then and do not be burdened again by a yoke of slavery." – Ephesians 5:1

Towards higher ground or higher level of hope, I ask myself where do I owe God repentance for feeling so familiar with him? Entitlement is a byproduct of pride. I so badly wanted to hold onto what God clearly said a firm no to. God makes no mistakes, nor does he apologize for his judgments; so, I must be obedient.

A common quote that pollutes our minds through feeding our egos in the church is "favor ain't fair". When we have a winning streak, we can begin to feel that we are one of God's favorites, without remembering that rain falls on both of the just and the unjust. Then, when challenging times come, we want everything to be good again instead of submitting and learning the lessons. The lessons, though difficult, can be blessings.

Our entitlement can lead us to believe that we are owed a certain income, a certain job position, a certain marriage, a certain lifestyle, and so on. We are not owed. We owe it all to the Lord, no matter if we are comfortable or uncomfortable in our lives. Are we sanctified when it's all good, but in the bar when it all falls apart? Are we praising God when we're on a roll, but cursing out everyone who we feel has wronged us when life gets hard? We must be consistent and obedient if we want to be true servants in Christ.

Pray, "God, please keep me humble and surrendered no matter my situation. When times are easy or hard, I serve You. I serve You, I serve You, I serve You. I am not owed anything, but I owe it all to You. Please help me to be the best servant to You that I can be. Please help me to serve You with my thoughts, actions, and habits. Thank You, Lord, for allowing me to be Your vessel. In Jesus name, Amen."

Day 21: God Deserves the Glory

My Minister in Training Process was a testing and pushing of my faith on all levels - financially, physically, mentally, emotionally, and of course, spiritually. I began this process without a job, yet still able to travel with my Pastor, serving at the altar, sowing seeds and learning to trust the providing attribute of God.

Next is the love aspect. I have learned, and I am still learning, to not trust in man, but in solely in God. There were so many moments where I longed for a tangible love and connection, yet I received rejection, deception, or nothing at all. He is my love and I am His (I believe this now). He's not disappointed or disgusted with me, it was me who was disgusted and disappointed in myself.

Many times, throughout this process I didn't know if I was going to make it, but I also knew the fight was worth everything. Where else can or will you go after you have already tried to move around what He has in front of you? I am grateful for the trials for they have made me stronger, more confident, and knowledgeable of who I am. The year of testing and trying has made me rely on the Holy Spirit as my friend and guide. He has taught me to not relent and trust where and what God says.

We received journals to write our revelations and thoughts in throughout this year. In the front, there was a message for us to carry with us throughout the journey. Inside of mine, it said, "more of Him and less of you." I truly appreciate the declaration and it helps me to appreciate the process so much more. When you know what God is trying to get out of you or produce through you it makes it more worthwhile.

I pray that you also experience a transformation through the short journey you have taken with this book. After my Minister in Training process, I breathed deeper and worshipped deeper. I recognized that deepening my journey with the Lord requires much sacrifice, practice, and selflessness. Knowing what I know now and experiencing Him how I have, I long to know Him in a new way. I pray for this for you as well. May you always hear the voice of our Lord and always follow only Him. To God to be glory, in the sun and in the rain. To God to be glory, in all things. In Jesus name, Amen.

Conclusion

My experience as a Minister in Training has been a long, disciplined, trying journey. Going into the beginning of the process, I had no idea what I had committed to until I saw the syllabus. The weekly readings, bi-weekly conference calls, 5 am prayers, and fasting dually with the MITs and the church both challenged and grew me as a Minister in Training.

I am grateful to have been able to relate to and empathize with the experiences of the other women on the MIT journey. Honestly, there were many times I felt like I was going through by myself because I initially undervalued those relationships. I am glad to have figured out the necessity of fellowship because otherwise, I do not believe I would have survived to the end.

Although this journey was an individual one, it is with the help of others that we make it out of the worse of circumstances. I cry thinking about how many times the other MITs put gas in my car, paid bills, interceded, watched my child, or simply listened as I wept from discouragement. It is those memories that I will cherish.

Major pressure points this year were learning to trust and hear God for myself. During this process, I had to walk away from people I wanted to hold onto and things that God said to release. The warfare was the most intense I have ever experienced but so were my encounters with God. It was on many road trips to support the ministry with my sisters that revelation, understanding, and knowledge was gained through acts of sacrifice, service, and sharing.

I look back at the pictures I took, the people that were there, and I don't recognize myself. It is as if a new woman has taken over my life. She doesn't have the same desires or feelings. Who knew how much one year could change your life? When I finally committed 100% of myself to God, he made me unrecognizable to myself. He afforded me the opportunity to forget and to forgive. He blessed me with a real second chance. I'm grateful and I shared that gratitude through writing this book to assist others with their journey to deepening their service to our Lord. Thank you for reading.

My Prayer for You

Reflecting on how I have been impacted as I continue this MIT journey, I realize that nothing I have been through will be wasted. God will use everything for his glory. My heartache, my pain, and my life lessons will all be used to minister. As I move on, my prayers are for your best future and your best opportunities. I pray that you be released from any pain from your past, blessed in every day of your present, and keeping God first every day of your future. In Jesus name, Amen.

About the Authors

Randryia L. Houston:
Consultant Randryia Houston is President of RLH Coaching & Consulting, a firm focusing on strategy development for visionary women leaders. Bestselling author of *I Almost Gave Up: Finding Faith in the Rubble of Brokenness* & *Shift: 20 Twenty Women Share Stories of Strength, Courage, and Succeeding Against the Odds*, Houston is passionate about women creating nonprofits, ministries, and businesses that speak to their true purpose. Blog contributor for sheownsit.com, Houston shares expertise and tips with entrepreneurs worldwide.

Houston began interest in social movements after a study abroad trip to Ghana, West Africa. Grieved by the educational disparities she witnessed for children the same age as her daughter, she was compelled to create The Pencil Project, a 501(c) 3 that has hand delivered over 300,000 pencils to primary and secondary school students in Ghana, Nicaragua, and Belize. She has been honored by Women in the World Foundation as one of six Super Charities Started by College Students, one of the ten most inspiring student activists, and Top 10 Game Changing Millennials of 2015 by the Global Millennial Conference. Houston's list of awards and international honors include features in the African Political and Economic Strategy Center and TelAfric Television Network.

Houston is an active philanthropist through the self-named Randryia L. Houston Endowment at the University of Houston Library, a Licensed Master Social Worker, Certified Christian Counselor and a licensed minister.

She resides in Houston, Texas with her 12-year-old daughter Ryann.

Rhonida A. Carter:

Rhonida A. Carter, author of *My Pearls Are Rare: A Collection of Poems Spanning from Brokenheartedness to Breakthrough* and CEO of Beauty, Wellness, and the Arts is a natural hair and fashion model who empowers young women to own their innate elegance and purpose via her mentoring and coaching.

Born in Agana, Guam, and raised in a military family, Carter is well-traveled and disciplined. At age 12, Carter held the three-time TaeKwonDo Junior Olympian Title as a red belt in San Diego, California. After relocating to Houston, Carter's passions evolved to singing, poetry, dance, NJROTC, and track and field, ultimately resulting in a full athletic scholarship to Texas A&M University in Kingsville; an athlete and artist at heart.

As a collegiate athlete, Carter's life and health drastically shifted due to multiple health complications. Diagnosed with a rare form of Mitral Valve Prolapse (MVP), a life changing heart condition, Carter discovered new depths of strength and determination. MVP created a unique opportunity to share and teach others how to face adversity and overcome regardless of self-image issues, diagnosis or limitations!

Carter holds a Bachelor of Business Administration in Accounting and is a licensed minister and Certified Christian Counselor residing in Houston, TX.

In 2017, Carter & Houston created the Pretty Face Heavy Weight brand. Pretty Face Heavy Weight is a faith based movement created to showcase that women are not only pretty but can produce vision, destiny, and purpose. Women are prophetic warriors who carry heavy weight in the spirit not trophies for the front rows of church pews. The movement has developed into a product line including the Hebrews 12 60-Day Devotional, Proverbs & Pillow Talk Devotional and Proverbs & Prosperity Affirmation Journal. For more information on books and apparel, check out www.prettyfaceheavyweight.com

Acknowledgments

Thank you to Bishop Tonya L. Davis and Dr. Della Provo for setting a firm, unshakeable foundation of servanthood and submission to the call of God. Thank you to our MIT sisters who shared in this journey of daily dying, sacrifice, and servitude.

www.ingramcontent.com/pod-product-compliance
Lightning Source LLC
Chambersburg PA
CBHW071646040426
42452CB00009B/1780